I Wish I Could
Steal the Sun

I Wish I Could Steal the Sun

Abbia Udofia

PARTRIDGE
A Penguin Random House Company

Print information available on the last page.

To order additional copies of this book, contact
Toll Free 0800 990 914 (South Africa)
+44 20 3014 3997 (outside South Africa)
orders.africa@partridgepublishing.com

www.partridgepublishing.com/africa

For Affiong Udofia

Contents

Castrating a Stubborn Truth

I Wish I Could Steal the Sun

Oaths & Indictments

Wreaths and Processions

Castrating a Stubborn Truth

Killing a Vulture

This hunter told me why and how he kills vultures.
Vultures foretell muted rites, hollow passages.
Vultures eat up the remains of time.
Vultures call up cheerful hyenas and scavengers
To dispose of invalid time and when he gives up
Vultures await our droughts
And pick our last breaths
With the wind mills of pretence.
So with a spear he waited among the millet stalks
And the valley of death
Like a lean scarecrow
Holding a famished shadow.
But we found his remains near the bloated field
Feeding a wake of ravenous vultures.

Outcasts

We are the blind ants in the cold mist of time.
Yet drawn by visions of our large-eyed earth.
Strained by livid love, harrying hope,
And revelations of barriers and humiliations.
Like the scruffy dress of destitute
Our devious fate hangs on our backs
From birth to grave.

The scents of evil are acknowledged
Like the fragrance of roses.
Outcasts in the well with endless echoes
A dream with smiling hangmen.
My necklace turns a serpent.

What the masquerade said

After the beheading, the head should be allowed to speak.
A lot would be garnered from the doomed and weak.
I am at a loss each time a pigeon is pulled by the neck
And the squirting blood sprayed across the broken wreak.

A Cockroach Chariot

Pride not in your elevated royalty,
It appears
You are on a cockroach chariot
And the chicken waits joyfully,
For your raffia convoy.

The Keyhole

The keyhole becomes a key trap,
And the door is shut from light,
The lyrical lure, calm, call of the sun,
Good air. Gone is the aimless arrow of hope
Dismissed is the bliss of bird song,
Dream-state, sun in a glass.
The innocence of a deer in the brook
Against the smooth hug of treachery.
The key forecloses evil unexpected
And grief and miseries unsuspected.

Friend

He once had a sweet friend
Never thought him as diehard fiend
Trust held both firmly like glue
But in truth this was not true.
Treachery twisted him like a snake
And feigned love they had at stake.
Like Cain, he drove him to murderous ends
Mindless of the evil his soul distends.

The Sun and I need Poetry Too.

The sun also reads poetry
Of legislated massacres
And decimated tribes
The sun also reads poetry of love
Taken with a pinch of venom
And the attendant watches with relish
As the served contorts in voiceless agony
And like a scotched plant, withers.
The sun needs poetry too
And some love to see his stolen light
From the cell of lost cremated heroes.

The Murder
(For Cecil the Lion)

I tried to bear the burden of his murder
From the moment of his passing.
Now the shots and beheading echo
In the blind halls of a bloody globe.

I am drawn to the mass of your passage.
Since I am but a dedicated bamboo
At riverside nestling the weary.
Time soon or later will pass
The marked green and the grey.
Now that we know
What the past and tomorrow taste
I wish I could be mourned like a king
And mark my grave with golden sceptres
And ornamented stones.

Ostracized

The ancient rite, infraction, infection
Dangle on your sullen neck, nailed
On your branded forehead;
An eternal letter of censure.
You are born outcast
Rejected, invalid, untouchable
On account of an ill-conceived avowal.

Lines of laughter

The broken lines of bliss and laughter
Are drawn smoothly like lines of grief
Whatever sweetness life may banter,
Agony breezes in soundless like a thief

Speaking honestly

He commences each interview with 'speaking honestly'
And we watch as he twists truth like a wand
In his magical hands.
He breaks facts like peanuts
And serves us butter of falsehood, value added
Beyond the searing realities of our cold hopes.

Inertia

She can't write poems particularly
When struck by the wool-touch thunder
And lightning of his love.
As she recuperates
In the intensive care chamber
Of her heart, she is shut out from all strokes..
She can't write poems to explain love
Found and lost; leaving love breathless,
On seeing love emerge like a goddess
From the house of vanishing; obliterating
Love and lovers slowly from sight
Like quicksand in the morass of rapture.
She has written and painted love of dying
And homecoming and unloving
Like rain and drought, light and void..
All exhibits eaten up by the long tongues
Of his love's ravenous inferno
Not leaving out the diviner's drum.

Fate

When the tiger eats the zebra and her foal
When the cobra swallows dove and eggs
And big drunk foot lands on ants and dregs
What fate befalls the blank common soul?

When green shrubs, tendrils seek sunlight
When blind storms kill greens in bitter bite
And the pigeon song ruined by the hawk
What fate befalls the foetus and his stock?

When the famished shark swallows sardines
And the shoal watch as he bloodily dines
When the ousted submits to heat and cold
Whence comes comfort, hope to the fold

All soon shall account to time and fate
On paths and lines and appointed date.
Miseries and pains will elongate or subside
The powerful and monstrous fate put aside

Inventions

The whispers between the master and maid
Presently will be in tablets, swapped in the open
Though the silence of the lady remains golden
Unaffected by indiscretions withheld or said

Castrating a stubborn truth

I wish I could castrate this stubborn truth
And dispose its sordid sour steaming broth

I will behead the disgusting disturbance
And sterilize the rampaging nuisance

I will break the neck of this aged rubbish
And delete its nauseating, felonious tarnish

I will blind and maim this restless rat
And terminate its muffling, stifling fart

Like a falcon I will snap this weaver bird
And chase it from its aberrant space, bed

This dogged annoyance should be castrated,
And its foppish diviners, proxies decapitated.

The Donkey's Parable

The burden may be heavy or light
Bright or gloom may be the sight
However far or nigh the destination
Hope and faith drive one's direction

Life's lesson may not open every door
May take you to hills and wet floor
What is late, soon will come to pass
However slow the toss of life's compass

One may be born to serve as a donkey
Not destined for pleasure's silky key
But a beast yoked for work and play
Yet walks with pride moving the hay

However burdened, flogged or derided
Life is uncruel, one serves blighted
Though none listens to plights and sighs
But the Creator has reasons for all dyes

Beggar Beautiful

Beggar beautiful, I present you
Neither silver nor gold.
I can only legislate your desiccation,
And colourful deletion.

The Tiger and the Deer

The starving tiger, out of sight stalking
The fields and night indifferent, unbulge
The prey roams praying for solace
The deer solves a nagging hunger
But there is lamentation in latter's domain

Incorruptible

In the webs and veils of evil holding all,
Heavy on hearts, heads, souls like gall
You stand clear, a lighthouse in the dark
For the weak, drained and broken rack

On the arduous path of righteousness.
While derision, malice, and impishness
Like hoary scarecrows taunt, intimidate
But your faith keeps our hopes obstinate

Far from the house of evil or perdition
Where sundry souls sadly malfunction
Turning swiftly, delightfully to the devil.
None faults you from the hill to the dell

Resilient to tempests of lucre and its flute,
Incorruptible, upright, virtuous, resolute
Keep your glorious honour above the gate
Storms and gales of evil cannot suffocate

You are the light of our peace and stores
You are salt and sweetness of our shores.

Jury Room

May be every heart should be like a tray
To display all evil borne by the wicked.
No matter how long the sun might stray
Shade shortly comes to the cold, naked

The nose smartly smells fart and filth
But declines detecting evil and treachery
Every divine face may not profess guilt
But inclined to fraud, murder, mockery

Cool is the water in the fish's head, tail
Cool is the house of the crab and snail.
The beautiful night has teeth as a shark
And she hides a long knife in her back

The accused is innocent from the flood
Of evidence, but the crowd wants blood
So like Pilate the Jury wash their hearts
And slickly dry them in the house of bats

Treachery

What makes a dog edgily barking all day
Keeps the goat cagey, and chewing its hay.
Water nurses the fish, water cooks the fish
Pardon fire, it's water that turns fish to dish

Near the Pulpit

Near the pulpit
A lingerie
Of unconfessed sins

Slave

From the dark and light of deformed shore
Abused like a slave shared by various masters
This space yet gratifies and favours hearts
Beyond measure of any used parch

In the silence of her eyes and plight
None can stand the sight of rent and fear
Against her fortitude and inclination
To delight her master regardless of pains

From head to feet her light is as midday sun
The gloom is perceived not by her
But other eyes dazed by the desiccated space
Yet time like an endless river refreshes

Whoever may wonder at pains and suffering
Need not bother at this bright and beautiful
She teaches the long lines of faith, hope, fortitude
Now we know why the rich resigns in tears
And princes chase faces in crystal dreams.

Death and the Golden Caps

They chased truth like a street thief
Far into the evil forest
For carrying a large mirror and gourd
Exposing their vulture hearts;
They hounded truth and hanged him
On the tallest palm;
Truth died smiling, head held high.
So they returned jubilating
With golden caps, eagle feather
And camwood beads to dance naked
In the village square.
Our cowries and gold vanished,
Our oil, grain and flowers dried,
As they ran us to blind swords
Of stone-hearted money lenders;
But truth subsists in fevered mangroves,
And bamboo shades; truth and death dine
In golden castles, corridors, chambers;
And sing joyfully
Of how golden caps beg not to die.

Truth

How sweet the curing sound, sight of truth
To the soft clarions of light and rectitude
How delightful the beauty, geniality of truth
To the bold bands of reason, integrity, virtue.

Truth dispels falsehood like oil on water,
Like a torch she clears the void of deception
Deceit took a fast sprint for a thousand years,
Truth took a day to bring him to the stake.

Falsehood's fire wrecked the house of truth,
Like the sphinx its was restored and refreshed.
How sweet the gentle sound and sight of truth,
Casting off searing veils of sleaze and blotch.

The Pianist

This fearless keyboardist taunts
The shameless searing shades,
The pianist fights pointless conflict
With an old sulking organ
Breaking walls, drawing tears
Metal strings hold hearts
And stitch them to hopes of heaven.

The Master and the Beast

They came with large shower caps like mushrooms
The path glittering in the distance with scenic mirage
The camel yelped with a smooth stab of the last straw
The master smiled. The road rode a two-headed horse
One proposing the master, the other disposing the beast.

I Wish I Could Steal the Sun

Snake Charmer

We are waiting on you, snake charmer
We see furious fangs fall
From the ghastly gums of simple snakes
And gorgeous ghosts hypnotize the stage
While you kiss your smiling serpents.
I am inclined to keep this appointment
And flaunt my cure and hypnosis
To eyes of my marinated consciousness

Poise

You hold on to dignity and purity
But we are dying of dishonour
And indiscretions and fatal indecisions.
Because of your light
The sightless rampages of locusts
The thoughtless violence of wolves,
Are receding, declining.
With your healing light, beauty comes
To our deformed faces, broken bones.
Honour like gold burnishes the heart
And like good perfume, fetches good air.

The Concubine

Your faith firmly, sedately
Twists mine like your pet.
This night like a python
Your love is drunken, fixated
Set for my dazed heart.
Is this alluring door opening
For my dismissal or interment?

Girl Destitute

The moon sketches our tattered shadows
Beyond the yawning gulping gallows
Like two cheerful moths, ill-fated
Submitting sins unabated
At the furious fire and noose yet sated,
Light-hearted, taking whatever follows..

The fishers

The best fishers
Return with blank nets
And beheaded mermaids

The abiku
Bury their heads in the field
And cry out with aches of love.

They are returning from the sea
That swallowed the happy hamlet
With gifts for the smiling orphans..

The Prodigal

Your sins are unsightly
Your face drawn out tautly
Your hands bear Lucifer's testaments
And share us his sweet sacraments

Eavesdropping on the Night

I eavesdropped on the testament of light
Between the gate keeper and the night.

The sun rises on the evil and upright
The rain comes on the virtuous or unjust
And time and wind may polish or rust
The banal and simple all glow or burst.
Whatever comes sleazy with the night
Soon will emerge to atone with the light

Sands

An elder once asked me to count the sands
For a clear audit statement of our ecology
And sociology.

But some sands are not countable,
Some fall within clay and loam,
Some stick under royal feet
Some are within presidential palaces
Guarded by dazed guards and wide eyed-dogs
Some are confined within wealthy estates
Restrained from common feet and eyes
Some are within covens,
Counted with fragmented beads
Some in segregated caverns
Restricted to Omerta divinations.

If Men were God

If men were God
The common humanity
Will starve and waste
Like abandoned scarecrows.
If men were God
They will hoard fresh air
And muffle us with heinous inflations
And huge tariffs paid for sunlight.
Like hounded hare
We will run into holes, atop trees
Estranged from our etherised earth.
If men were God
The planets will be snatched
From their celestial spaces
And hidden in monstrous pouches.
If men were God
The rain will fall on selected roofs,
And lawns while we eat soil
Like ants, earthworms, bush rodents.
If men were God
The powerful will corner us each
Into their large pens and slaughtered
For pointless pride and carnivals

Our Husband is Richer than Yours

Our husband is richer than yours
We are wealthy within and outdoors
So keep your long trout, rags indoors
See our alluring faces, backs, braces
Far beyond what your man graces

Our husband is lovelier than yours
So hide your unsightly miseries, yaws
Come for our lavish hand-outs, favours
Even with your sad husband or in-laws
Your kith will meet our huge stores

Our husband is stronger than yours
He holds public purse and doors
Tall and stout men run his errands
Some bearing his kolanut, snuff bands
Like ants running chores in the sands

Our husband is fatter than yours
Come away to our royal tours
He can eat an elephant at a go
His belly is an ocean, a grand cargo
There is space whatever you throw.

Thief by Mistake

I am a thief by mistake
I am a lifter by default.
How tactless my hand in the soup pot?
How was I to know the treasure bag
From the balcony wasn't mine?
Forgive my thoughtless hands
The sun shines on elephants and ants
And palaces share with common serfs.

I am a thief by error.
I am a crook by slip.
Was the edgy goat I led away
From the crossroads, yours?
O, sister forgive me.
Was the noisy chicken I seized
From the street corner, yours?
O, brother pardon me.
Which teeth asked to keep meat
Will not draw or savour a sheet?
Which bee asked to fetch nectar
Will not taste sweetness so dear?
Forgive my slippery fingers.
Pardon my stealthy legs.

Do not run in doors at my coming.
Do not speak quietly, abusively
When I walk the street.
I am a thief by mistake.

I am a thief by error.
I turned over a new leaf.
Ah, what is this treasure box
Again doing in my pocket?
Come on, whose jewels and trinkets
Are these anyway?

Father Remember

Father remember me while you eat our ancestral ox
Remember me while you clear out our family bull,
Remember me and those after.
Remember those who came before you
Who were never guided by the lure of profligacy,
Who were never blinded by glamour of blood wealth.
Remember me while you drink off our winery
And exhaust the yams in the family barn.
Why are you sending our fertile clouds
To rain in distant plains?
Why are you speaking silently
With sly strangers in our sacred shrines?

I wish I could steal the sun

I wish I could steal the sun,
And the moon and the stars.
I wish I could have everything,
And leave every one nothing.

I wish I could steal the sun,
And all the lights and sights
So the king, queen, and all
Would plead for my favour.

I wish I could steal the Moon.
Stars, and the planets,
I wish I could steal the seas,
The oceans and even the rains

My wealth will bring the high
And low to my door seeking
Water and milk from my barns
To quench their thirst.

I wish I could steal the night
And make the earth without rest
Like the restless guests in hell
To plead for space and sleep

I wish I could steal the sun
And have fun beyond the sun.

My Father Tells Lies

Lies are not good, lies are not decent.
But father lies to me, he lies to me.
I know father lies to me, I know he lies
May be he does not know he lies
May be he doesn't know I know he lies.
Everybody knows my father lies.
Father lies to me and it makes me cry.
Father don't tell me lies anymore
Father don't tell me lies again
Everybody knows you are a liar.
Mother does not like your lies.
Grand pa does not like your lies.
They call you bad names for lies.
Father don't tell me lies anymore.

A Bribe

It's a favour paying gratification
Before your delayed birth
Doctors are on strike
And a kind-hearted nurse
Delivers your death.
A curtain drawn
To hide the light-fingered clerk
Now I must pay an inducement
For your burial
Even the mortuary attendant
Like Eden's serpent, suggests
The forbidden for this peculiarity.
He needs practical sums urgently
To fix our dark anticipations.

The Queue

A queue of the spent in the superannuity office.
In the superannuity office a line of the frail
In the pensions office
A long tired queue of the spent for pensions.
How can anyone not see this line
Like a line of give-aways for charity?
How can the watchful earth not see this line
With the milky softness of their conscience?
How can anyone be oblivious of the widening
Silent queue of heroes and veterans and elders?
In the busy pensions office
There is a long line of the old, hungry and frail
Waiting and sighing
Seeking substance for their wasted labours.

Bearer of Lies

Bearer of lies welcome
From your endless peregrination.
Bearer of lies you tell lies sweetly
More than the lure of the sea sirens
You told lies and exhausted lies
From the house of lies.
You depleted lies from the trees of lies
You ate up lies from the land of lies
You drained lies from the sea of lies.
You told lies amiably even mermaids
Emerged from the seas joyous.
You told lies perfectly
Even eagles fell from their great heights
You told lies and worms and grubs
Danced to celebrate your shrewdness.

You told lies dexterously even legends
Of lies wondered at your industry
You told lies and beasts left the wild
You told lies and fish left the deep
You told lies the wind forsook our shores.
Bearer of lies welcome to our hamlet,
Welcome to our innocent space.

The Drinkard

I had my wine in Itodo and the city celebrated me like a war hero
I took my wine in Ibiko and I was awarded a national medal
I got my calabash in Ndaha and I won myself a titanic trophy
I drained a pot in Mbaha and the king awarded me his lovely
Princess
Let us drink and kill our trackless woes
Let us drink and drive off our pains or foes

I drank my wine in Itigi and the landlord
Forgave my long rents
I drank my wine in Ntoho and my creditors
Deleted my endless debts
I had my wine in Ntaka and the tax man
Wrote off my levies
I took my wine in Udehe and the medicine man
Gave me a lightning amulet
Let us drink and kill our miseries, woes
Let us drink wherever time's river flows

I took my wine beyond the endless seas,
The white queen granted me a mansion
I took my wine in distant islands
And the King awarded me a plaque,
I took my wine in the woodlands
And got myself a goddess
I took my wine beyond the golden shores
And won a bag of gold.
Let us drink and shame our many foes
Let us drink and merry whatever life throws

The Face

The sort of comportment
That holds Angels
Draw hearts to your knives
With venom sweetened
With your soulful smiles

Oaths & Indictments

Condemned

Condemned like a fly pressed under glass.
The sleepy jury believed the eye witnesses
So the blameless defendant was deleted
Like a wrong word from a beautiful page
Like a fly snapped by the frog's long tongue.
We return to a burgled home.
A loud juror is indicted by the grand jury.

After the Meeting

After the meeting
The dusty feet go home
Far from the dinge
Of sweet tongue birds

Promises were doled out
Like hot soups
By the miracle master
Dry lips are licked
In anticipation, sweetness
Of the golden aftermath
Of our foretold feast

Every blade, bird, beard
Wait for refreshing returns
Of soulful pledges
Of a milky morn
Nourishing noon
Blissful dusk.

May comets, fluorescents
Fly with our hearts
And not sink
With agonies of dawn.

Rituals last market day
Are yet unrequited
Messenger doves

Unreturning, affirming
The obtuse lobes
Of distorted divinations

May our pious priests
And gatekeepers
Not loose or break
Our ancestral beads
And grow light fingers

May the awaited sun rise
beyond the dark horizons
And healing dawn draw
Hope in our first steps
Beyond the soothing dews

Indictment

I am dressed in black, the bride of death.
I carry leaves on my clean shaven head
For stray goats to have their go.
I, the bride of the departed.
Indicted to explain innocence.

I must share bed with the ascended
And a good drink of his bath water
To confirm my debated blamelessness.
I dance through the village in black
Announcing my defoliation, sequences
Of guilt. Then the oaths of seven shrines
And mourning in veiled rooms, chambers
Of gloom, hanging halls, and lethal passages.
Death sits astride.
Taking noxious notes, lines of the conscripted.

Truth and Reconciliation

Truth and Reconciliation insist
The bloodied aggrieved overlooks weals and scars.
Wailings in broken, distressed hearts
Should be forgotten on the plateau of harmony.
The long lines of granite stones
The countless sculls stacked high up
In the dark scarlet chambers of cruelty
Are drawn behind the false veil of forgiveness.
Mother hen turns away sadly
From her crying chick in the eagle's beak.
The pier and bier must reconcile pains.
Blood of babies slaughtered at the nursery
Unknown thousands cremated for time.
The contrite cobra throws up a dead deer.

The wrath

The wrath has come atoning
And sins less becoming.
But the great fire
Must consume the believer
And review the dreadful errors
Thrown up and broken indoors.

The Oath

Now that the sworn declarations have been made
To delighted compatriots, remember o priest,
The famished faces outside the golden corridors.
Now that solemn promises have been delivered
To boisterous witnesses, remember o priest,
The searing demands of the restrained.
Now that the last foot has departed
The sacred square, remember o priest,
The calling, sighing behind the dark groves.
Now that the swearing-in feasts and banquets
And dances are over, remember o master,
The prayers and pleas among hungry homesteads.
Now that fresh oaths have been exchanged,
Deposited in divine recesses, remember o wayfarers
Traumas and miscarriages of former seasons.
The once beautiful spouse
Has gone and returned from countless altars
And tossed by grooms drunk, riotous,
and those sober, reflective, pious.
The pride of these expanses lie desolate,
Derided by her former maids and butlers,
Broken by her snuff bearers, eccentric eunuchs.
Remember o master the silent pleas of the desolate
Remember o priest the rumblings among the quiet.
Like figures in the dust, we crouch for last bells,
We await refreshing calls of new priests for full feasts
And chase off bandits pricing homeless hunchbacks.

Distant Flames

Like firemen waiting, chasing infernos,
Seeking long tongues of fire, dominoes
Hearts extricated from their restful homes
But stultified in paper cones, domes
We know not ourselves but distant flames
And seem not to know our familiar names

The Echoes

You despatched my messages like void calls
In the valley of muted echoes
Your face lingers in the cold recess of my mind
With Hellenic smiles
That sent kingdoms to vain wars
But our love, a frozen relic, a broken tree
In the storm of time
Raises unquenchable fires
Consuming the forests of our doubts
And lawns of our disbeliefs.

Expiation

The medicine man has lost his head
In the shrine of sculls, shadows
That call for returns, atonement.

Divination from the chief priests
Is blank like a moonless, starless sky
Seeking foretelling from mouths of babies.

The witch doctor saves his dinner
For the coven's cat,
How did water get into the snail's guts?
What spells the saint and supplicant?
What holds the priest and patient?
What breaks chords of the ancient grove
What seizes notes of the master's flute?

What vanishes abandons the waiting.
The expected diminishes the expectant
In the shrouded shrines of expectation.
The returning reiterates previous horrors,
Speaks of the mourning of the dismissed.

Like crabs at riverside in and out of their holes
Dishonoured brigands search for expiation.

Poet Write This

You write so beautifully and exquisitely,
That poems sing and brighten your pages
You write so strikingly and intricately
That lyrical lightning flashes
And lights up your brilliant books.

Have you written of the dead children washed ashore
From the capsized boats and dugouts
Their parents contorting in endless sequences of agony?
Have you put down lines on the child soldiers,
Running the streets, murdering parents and family
And the phantom bliss in startled eyes of their dead fellows?
Have you written on the blown babies born in the fields
And taken away by joyous jackals and wandering wolves?
Have you seen their remains and cords despatched
By ravenous fangs to waiting vultures?

Have you written of the tearful thousands
Crossing the crimson Mediterranean seeking
Doves and olives from heart-folded shores
Or those drowning in waves of terror, blown away
By bland devices borne delightfully by toddlers?
You write beautifully and exquisitely,
That poems sing and brighten your pleasant pages
You write strikingly and intricately
That lightning flashes, lights up your enthralling rhymes.
Write this poet, write
The land bleeds and begs for your absorbing verses.

Alibi

The ladders have fallen
And faces in open masks
Make home runs to catch
The missing distance.

She draws logarithms
In the recesses of my soul;
Each day, her face
Like dove wakes me,
Insisting I handle her
Like earthenware, like pottery
For the gods.

I am the inquisitive moth
Buried in the wax's warm solace.

Fly, fly, O heart,
Hold on to wet clouds,
Fly, fly, O soul, find solace in the wind,
Find warmth in blind lights, arms
In the cold distance of the absconding light

The Old Treat

She didn't make the heart beat
Dance, dream like the old treat?

Was it the fresh dew girl
Who emerged in a whirl
Whose mercuric smiles,
Took you to clouds and miles?
Was it the lovely verse star
Whose beauty flung eyes afar,
Making priests dreamless
And poets sleepless?

Life like diamond
Will go on profound,
From thirst, rain, green, ash,
Heart will flourish with a bash
And joy will vanish in a flash

The Loop

Were you the one at the door, garden last night
Making pantomimes with the sighing shades?

Were you the primus, blindfolded night,
With larks evolving needles of passage?

You the skipping shadow in the dark distance
Asking colours of pretence, essence of sense.

This night, I attend the temple and sit alone
Thinking about the fading flowers, sulk stars.
The wind is cold, I sit with sleepy candles
In the darkness, the angels decline calling me.

Our children are going to war

The children are going to war
In beautifully starched uniforms
They are going to war,
To stay our brilliant elders from venoms holds
To prevent deranged elders from spinning evil,
From breaking the aged gourd of harmony
And picking the splinters in distant homesteads,
Retrieving our umbilical cords in strange potsherds.

At the train station

In the coffee room
She sat reading journals,
Cross-legged.
Two lovers emerged
From the din
Like dragon flies
On the face of the station's stream.
She read beyond the lovers
And asked me to tea
Cross-eyed, reading..

Butterfly

Butterfly, delight not in the sunlight
Someone is calling
For rains.

The Silence

The silence of the wailing night pleads.
The indifference of the groaning day speaks.
Lie on discarded hopes of a vanished mother,
Lie on shredded robes of a possessed mother.
The truth of hurried footfalls seeks you some light
The rustling in blank paths brings you oil..
Where the matcheted silence breaks
With a grenade of love, affections.
In the distance a fire fight of ancient bile
Where the bloated venom of articulated blasts
Detonate the ancient pretensions and deceits
Holding us as one, breaking us as cookies.
The silence of the shrugging paths weeps for you.

O, heart at sundown of beginning,
O, soul at dearth ending.
Rise at intersections of reason,
At the penumbra of unreason.
The divination of doves, pigeons expiate for you
The rituals of egrets and owls atone for you
Away from valleys of blood, of death growling
Like famished hounds seeking devouring

The silent songs of unborn faces implore you
The echoing silence of gone faces beseech you
Camwood, scarlet lines on faces, paths of reckoning
Predictions on light walls, on blind rafters
Where bliss is celebrated like aged funerals

Of living, of evolving, of budding.
The quiet of green graves entreat you
Whose songs are smoother than cherubims
Waiting for righteous homecoming.
The quiet of wailing widows, orange orphans
Whose momentous mourning shakes the earth
Like a tree in the path of a hurricane;
All plead for atonement, penance.
O heart, unhide from the chambers of fireflies oblivious
Of the night's knives and fangs
O heart loose your ostrich robes from sands of pretence
These tears and hearts plead for expiation, propitiation.

The fire

The fire has blown off the wind
And the palace is in flames.
Firemen run seeking amends of the gods.
Medicine men crouch on divination mats
Lost in the clouds of fire.
The fire has blown off the wind
We are naked belly and back
At the swollen shrines of infractions, infections.

Strange Fellows

In present times, foggy
The face is concealed from the self
In folds and glaucoma shutters
The self is concealed from the self
By cataracts of deleted consciousness
And the two strange bedfellows
Supposed sweet fellows
Are confirmed sour, detached
By the heart's decree
Absolute.

The Man who stole the Witch Doctor's Wife

The sly fellow took the witch doctor's wife
And the weird one in shame took his life
Though to most sights this was unpleasant
The old one lost his wife to his sly servant.
It remains a recurring tale though all at sea
Of how the kind hearted healer lost his space
To schemes and tricks of the lowly employee
Surely evil will burst like wild weeds to its face
The servant stole the master's wife and trade
But ended up creating more witches than cure
It's complex what a man could from life endure.
Trust may cut smooth, deeper than knife or blade

The Estuary

The bay floats like oil on water.
Like a raft on oil
Yesteryears miseries indorsed.
Fumes splayed, validated.
Fishes desert the rivers
And soil flout the farmer
And the air contravenes breaths.
This is the famously rich estuary
Of dancing stilts
Of glorious obscurity
Of a smiling gloom..

Voices from a Construction Site

I finished loaves of bread with the aroma
From my neighbour's loaded kitchen.
In the delightful dream I closed a gourd
With the crummy fatback tax collector.
I the coffin maker, business has a limp, lull,
Men are becoming parsimonious with death.
The man with missing dentures, bony chest
Wants to compete in a bone-eating contest
The foppish stranger visited our latrine once,
But over-fed our large suck-away to the brim.
The other man farted smoothly and afflicted us
With strange plagues, and virulent virus.
We all know the legendary trick of keeping
A meat lump in the cheek, then declare it lost.
The vain wife called the mute husband, fool
Man brought in a lovely maid brook-cool.
Every worker deserves his wages, not rags
So Master, take not our wages for granted
Is it true you were with the King's daughter
Last night behind the village square?

Nicodemus
For Innih

We cautioned your bare feet sermons.
We protested your nightly prayers
Forged only for the most beautiful.
We objected your mountain top
Ascent with the hitch hiking princess
Claiming your visions confirmed her
As our new Debora priestess.

Then the muffled outcry
And you vanished
Appearing only nocturnally
Affirming all must be born again
The new-borns chasing untold histories.

What and where is truth, teacher?
We are old, can we be reborn
As fresh eggs conceived
At the bank of a lost river?
Who fathers the old tendrils
Forged by the drunk ancestors?

Is it true that spectres are reborn,
Turning the living to gnomes
And nymphs to the living
And we are mere snuff boxes
For our mumbling forebears
Eating the re-born's cocoyams
With oil in closets of phantoms?

Termites

The rains brought them to our lanterns
Hung low and high in hearts
And we scampered in the rush
Of the surplus
More than our waited annuities.
We are in the open chasing
Termites
With the dying night and lanterns
The elders are woken, broken,
Waiting with dusty crockery
Of hearts eaten by termites
Marinated with tasteless cotyledons.

Waiting

We are yet waiting for our lost daughters
We have lived with muted dreams for seasons
Blown up by nightmares of their tender smiles,
And the gentle calls to fetch them home.
We are waiting for our stolen daughters
Drowning in the sea of blankness, void
And in the blankness of our waiting
We see their faces like candles in the void
But we die waking up to our invented sanities
And inhibited psychosis.

Famine

In farms green and infinite
Droughts are harvested
In large bowls
Infants return late,
Empty
To the cold fireplace ..

The chicken war

First it was a chicken donated
By a visiting officer
To two puffy chiefs.
Then the dispute revolved on
The honour of killing the fowl.
Debates went left and right
And centre and left again
The matter was unresolved.
A native priest was summoned
To settle the contention.
He threw a cowrie and another
The lot fell on the left.
The next storm was on
Whose right was the chicken head
A salacious part of the barbecue.
Tempests rose on the gizzards
The chicken thighs and chest.
Calm never came.
So they went to war.
The thunder and lightning
Harvested hundreds of heads.
When it abated the chicken was gone.
Not even the bones were left
For the starving children.

The dragon tattoo

Whose colours and lines
Blink on your chest
Speaking fire
Of forgotten affections?

Simulation

I ran and drew all the energies
On your affection
Inserting the frolics, diversions
Of love and passion.
Then you confronted me
With a cautioning card for simulation

When Madmen Seize Divination Trays

When madmen seize divination trays
And trifle with our ancient chests
And sport with our aged gems
And roast fertile foetuses of tomorrow
And burn sacred shades, figures of faith
What relief do we crave
From our malignant markets?
What bliss from our sullen squares
What succour from our hounded homes
What sanity in our pompous parliaments
What progress in our crocodile cabinets?
When madmen seize divination trays
And tear our ancestral beads,
What honest heart and eloquent eyes
Will direct our melting hearts?
What divine hands will find our faltering feet
And mend our impractical sky and earth?

February, 2003

Cecilia

When the rainstorm comes in the night
She comes with dreams of Cecilia.

Last night it was rain and her storm.
Cecilia appeared regale, resplendent
A queen of his tapestried dreams

She made him run rivers like a dragon fly
She made him run the waterside like a mudskipper
The canoe men and fishers wondered at his indiscretions.

The first night she made him bear his ransom
And fetched dowries of her former suitors
The second night she presented his drunk head
To head hunters but the rainstorm rescued him

Cecilia was there in the folds of the night
The rain, storms, ransoms, dowries, priests.
They are at her uncanny grove
She chants her love and attraction
She fetches priests and head hunters for beheading

Wreaths and Processions

Processions

Like ants silent, sedate
As on the devil's date
Their faces dry different
Like bodies recovered late
From a frozen sea, irreverent.

You Wonder why I Cry for Love

Remember men who for love lost their broken being
And sicken senses in the genial thoughts of lost love?
Remember women who abandoned solace for trauma
Clinging on the delicate threads of gracious love.
You wonder why I cry for love?
What sweetness oozes from the bulging beehive
What maddening fondness can draw
Venomous volcanoes from the sea of affection
Remember hearts blown up by love perpetually,
Guided by hollow heaths of unbroken promises.
But then love must be worn like a blame mark
In a labour camp or a death row train,
Stuck to the chest and self-descriptive
Of the final solution to a difficult scourge.

The Wreath Bearers

Weep not departed, rather mourn
and mark your immanent portions.
Celebrate ash and earth like your hearts.
Allow not the wind song of this black procession
Drown you like bees in a gourd of wine.
So dress your fate gorgeously like onion bulbs,
Delightfully for the sizzling wrath to come.
The maggots are sober in their silent banquet.

Ghosts Rocking a Bench

With drought came a monstrous mist blinding
the sulking sky and snooping earth.
With thirst came bandit boils, miseries
Like Pharaoh plagues.
We survived quicksand afflictions defying cures.
After the tenth plague and pains
Purple haired-ghosts sat rocking a bench
Near the dry forgotten well.

Bones

Is this the one who strengthened the restless stallion?
Is this you that held the golden crown of great warriors?
Is this the smoking tail that frightened
Even tigers and hyenas
And hounded them beyond the land beyond
The whispering forests?
Birds now defecate on these scared bones.
Rats play hide-and-seek in your dry dead hands.

Anticipation

She takes her bath late in the night
Her hair well laid and apportioned
The make-up bright and assertive.
Then her night clothes are princely
The perfume astounds even the wind.
She insists she passes in honour
And avoid the family a pointless burden
Of an unreasonable undertaker.
She prefers to depart in a full moon
With the raft of shuttling ancestors
Or backed like a baby across restless rivers
Suckled with the earth's long breasts
On restful chests of one-eyed mermaids.

The Burial

The grave diggers are gone, processions all gone
The choir and mourners and the dead all done.
There will be shorter but misty paths home
There will be quieter, solemn rites back home.
Feet lighter, wondering, and hesitating roam
Hearts and heads levitate with gory grief's foam.
Hymns, choir fervent as rites on judgement day
Bear burdens of a hunchback on the murky loam
Oblivious but pass now, again in black and grey

Wool Gathering

She was returning from wood-gathering
In her heart a yoke heavier than the faggots
Under her bare feet ancestral oaths unfulfilled
In her blank eyes onion tears laden, unshed,
She sang to the bush path, voice like a child
About an old woman once a dazzling girl
She came gold cladded but cast off near nude.
The chorus returned an old man, then toddler
Now a laughing stock near the village gate
All affirmed their sad fate will never abate.

Dirge

Sing the dirge loudly, louder than Kigali
In the concrete bliss of stacked sculls.
Sing the dirge loudly, soulful like Monrovia
Muffled by the strange viral affliction
Even the dead beg not to be touched or mourned.
We are worms, we are birds, our nests
Are beyond us, now we fly endless.
But how far from this cold terminus is heaven?

Ogunpa

In the rampaging flood
Like an unforgiving debt gleaner,
The hands of a baby holding leaves.
Ogunpa, even a child must atone
Evil, indiscretions, distress beyond stone?
Child, sleep well, permit a tear drop
To change precepts from our mountain top.
Like Moses' devoted sister
I will pick you at the foot of the river.

The Colony

In the colony
Of afflictions incurable
Death,
Death song
Endless

The victim

The victim from the suicide blast is dead.
The heavy wife and silent children unfed
They look to the distance for his return
But only the late footfalls come forlorn
In the cold recesses of blown hearts
The victims are waiting, silent outcasts

Hit and Run

One is incapable of telling what should have been
Not finding words or self in what was seen.
On immediate impact of the hit and run
Against the sketches and crimson sun
The young girl lies dead on the tar
Not too far from the faded zebra.
The teenage girl is down in endless steep
Cold and flat as if in drunken sleep,
The toddler brother nudges her to wake up
Oblivious of this fatal fate and broken cup
The gathering eyes and feet watch arms akimbo
Some giraffing with snacks and food on the go
Sad and incapable of telling what should have been
Some finding themselves in what they have seen

A baby in the well

A baby fell from her mother into a well
A sight sense and sanity cannot tell
Mother wept, called where her baby fell
But got blank echoes from the deep cell

Tombstones of Idoro

Pray for us stones,
Pray for us.
Your vows and pledges
Are firm on the face of heaven
Pray for us..

When he drowned

When he drowned
The sea brought him back
With sands on his lips
With leaves on his feet
Twigs on his clenched fists.
When he drowned
Shadows brought him back
With light in his eyes
With camwood on his body.
When he drowned
The moon brought him back
With songs of night birds
With the cool wind before dawn
With long sighs of the undead.
When he drowned
Dreams brought him back
As a boy in the sand, play-acting
As a ghost rest-place searching.

Broken

The day is loaded with tears
The night burdened with griefs
Faces turning against walls
Frightened of friendly faces
Hands hold shadows in self-belief assurance
The road is filed shrunken, begging, dying faces
Waiting for the last angel
Running the last days anointing the quick.
Priests kiss their divination trays
And merge themselves with sighs,
And gaze through hearts like globules
Not knowing why royals die and beggars live
Whose footprints run through here?
Whose sighs yet hold and break our space?
Whose songs, whose laughters are broken?
Who remains sun gazing, moon sighting,
Not knowing why we grief or laugh
Not knowing why we live or die?

In the Shadow of the Storm

An old woman in the shadow of the storm, said some prayers.
A ghost sauntered through the gloom with a placard.
Angelus in the hut of horrors
And the smile is leaked off her face
Like butter by a hungry bear.

The heart of Poverty

In the repugnant heart of cruel poverty
A pigeon in distress.
The groom's eyes has a drop of tears.
The rain of drought and starvation refreshes
And vultures sing a chorus of underfed banquet.

A Dream

There was a song and a dream
A song not for mourning.
But eyes came sulking, tears broken
Braking everyone like firewood
In the soft cold hands of harmattan.
Songs and dreams discovered us
Burnished fossils in some getaway picnic.

I died in a dream and it was blissful,
In the land of no remembrance
The land lacking pains and hunger,
Just beautiful dreams.
The wind whistled
Of the mysteries of songs and dreams.
Can there be recalls of songs, dances?
Can there be memories of light and rains?
The sea returns its colourful catch
The earth throws up scarlet accounts
Birds sing of our horrifying muteness
And trees bow in prayer to hooded axes.

The Valley of Death

In the morning blindness, I shot a widow,
A homeless variant of the discarded.
She appeared like a bush rodent
And her sight demanded taking her down
Mercifully to grant her rest.
But widows are forever.
I wasn't simulating the church massacre.
For we all shall survive beyond the valley of evil,
Beyond the shadow of death.

For a Baby Poodle on her Death Day

The week long cry set it apart
From the litter
And slowly like a shrinking sprout
It withered. On her naming day
She departed. Cold, black eyed,
Mouth wide, eyes closed as in deep
Meditation. Blood from her mouth
As if returning the pains of her birth.

The Toast

The man with the last cup raised it up for a toast.
Against the thunders of the watchman's loud boast
But it all came to naught with the soft call of a ghost.

Printed in the United States
By Bookmasters